The RICH LIFE

Managing Wealth and Purpose

SUSAN LATREMOILLE

The RICHLIFE

Managing Wealth and Purpose

SUSAN LATREMOILLE

FIRST EDITION
Susan Latremoille
181 Bay St., Suite 3910
Toronto, ON M5J 2T3
Phone: 416-969-3026
Email: info@TheLatremoilleGroup.com
www.TheLatremoilleGroup.com

Library and Archives Canada Cataloguing in Publication

Latremoille, Susan, 1951-
The richlife : managing wealth and purpose / Susan Latremoille.

ISBN 0-9781401-0-9 (bound).--ISBN 0-9781401-1-7 (pbk.)

1. Finance, Personal. 2. Self-actualization (Psychology) I. Title.

HG179.L37 2006 332.024 C2006-904016-8

Book Design/Layout: Olena Sullivan, New Mediatrix
Cover Graphic: Suzanne Noga
Printed in Canada

To Nicholas and Sarah, with all my love

TABLE OF CONTENTS

INTRODUCTION

> *"To live, to love, to learn, to leave a legacy. This mission statement from Stephen Covey could easily have been my father's. He lived each day to the fullest. He loved his family, his heritage, his connection with the outdoors. He never stopped learning – from philosophy to magic, from woodcarving to the Internet. And he left a legacy in Peterborough, at Camp Ponacka on Baptiste Lake, and in the hearts of everyone gathered here today to mourn his passing."*

So began the eulogy that I delivered at my father's memorial service. The service was a celebration of his life, and as I looked out over the people before me, I could feel his presence.

His presence was evident in the faces of his family, my family. In the faces of the men whose lives he had touched, men whose dreams could easily have been quashed when they were youngsters but who were now living their dreams, thanks to him. In the faces of his friends who were no doubt remembering the particular ways he had touched their lives.

During his life, my father and I did not always see eye to eye. But since his death I have come to understand the importance of the legacy he left me. He instilled in me the ability to believe in myself, and because of that I have conquered my fears and accomplished things I hardly dreamed of doing.

I see now that my father's life was a life well lived, and that he left a legacy for others as well. And I am struck with a sense of urgency about creating the kind of legacy my father left. But that is not all. I also feel strongly that the value of my legacy will depend, at least in part, on how successful I am in encouraging others to come to their own sense of purpose and fulfillment, to be as deliberate and passionate about the important things in their lives.

This book is intended as a crystallization of insights about the interplay of wealth and personal fulfillment – insights that I have been fortunate enough to garner in a financial management career that spans a quarter of a century. I call the perfect balance of wealth and personal fulfillment the RichLife, and I hope that this book might inspire others to find this balance.

Chapter 1

FAMILY HISTORY, THE SOURCE OF MY RICHLIFE INSPIRATION

My Father's Story

My story begins with my father's story because he kindled in me the fire of his passions, his values, and his vision of life.

Innsbruck, Austria, 1917. My father was born with a silver spoon in his mouth. Not literally, of course, but his parents had achieved substantial financial and social status. His father was a lawyer by education, a banker by profession, and in his later career was transferred to Prague to assume the duties of a bank president.

His mother became a paragon of Prague society who devoted herself tirelessly to the artistic and cultural life of the city. She loved nothing better than discovering emerging artists; she would further their careers by offering them her financial support and by introducing them to others who became their patrons. She planned the frequent and lavish entertaining that my grandfather's position required, and she was noted as a consummate hostess. And all the while, she kept track of the many details of day-to-day life in her home, with a guiding finger in every aspect of running a mansion with servants, a butler, a chauffeur, and a governess. This was the milieu in which my father and his three siblings lived as children.

My father always loved the outdoors, and in a decision that was somewhat surprising for a young man raised in such circumstances, he had decided by the age of sixteen that he wanted to become a farmer. His family supported his decision, and although his own father died that same year, my father went off to agricultural school, and his family invested in a large farm that was to become his when he finished his studies.

Shortly after he finished school, however, Hitler began his march through Europe. The Nazi movement was strong, powerful, and life-threatening. My father was a Jew. He knew his chances of survival at the hands of the Nazi government were slim, and so he abandoned his aspirations, left his home, and narrowly escaped from Czechoslovakia to Holland on a counterfeit visa. His Uncle Robert met him there with the financial means to get him to England.

The war destroyed many things, but it did not destroy his dream of farming. While in England he heard about a piece of property in Ontario, Canada, that had once been a fruit farm but was now derelict. No stranger to risk, he bought the property for $1,000, sight unseen, and then he headed off for a new life in Canada.

To make ends meet in his new country, my father worked in a basket factory at night while he struggled to restore his farm to its former flourishing state. When the war ended, he enrolled in the University of Western Ontario and took both an undergraduate and a Master's degree in philosophy.

At university, he found love in the form of a beautiful girl from Exeter, a small town in southwestern Ontario. After they married, he graduated and took a job teaching philosophy at Trinity College at the University of Toronto, where he also earned his Ph.D. in philosophy.

His passion for nature refused to stay dormant. Using part of the proceeds from the sale of the fruit farm, he purchased for a few hundred dollars an abandoned camp on

Baptiste Lake, south of Algonquin Park. The trip from Toronto to the camp entailed driving for an entire day over dirt roads and then taking a half-hour trip across the lake in a small boat – a gruelling journey, but for him it was all part of the adventure.

My father thought that boys who lived in cities led a constrained life. He thought they ought to be able to experience and appreciate life outside the urban world, to inhabit at least for a while a place where heat came from wood fires and not from a furnace in the basement, where trees grew in a forest instead of in neat lines along a city street. From his own experience, my father knew about the importance of community and sharing, values that he had learned himself from living on the farm.

A passion for nature, and especially for the wilderness, was in his blood. He felt strongly that only in the magnificent outdoors could a person fully appreciate the magnitude of the natural world and the relative significance of what was created by human hands. His overriding dream was to create a summer camp for boys so that children from the city who had never been in the wilderness or experienced living outdoors could gather together to learn outdoor skills.

My father had a great deal of respect for people who lived in a rugged natural environment. He appreciated the fact that they relied on their own resources more than those who lived in towns and cities. In the country, my father said, people respected what they were given and wasted nothing. They hunted for food and used everything – he told me about an old-timer he had met who had even used the skin of a loon to cover a cushion for his boat seat.

So my father created Camp Ponacka on Baptiste Lake in 1947, and he and my mother canvassed their neighbourhood, knocking on doors to find boys whose parents would be willing to send their sons off for a month to the wilderness. In its first year, the camp attracted 20 boys.

Camp Ponacka was my father's mission, his passion, his dream. He created a world where boys in their formative years could visit for four weeks a summer and have experiences that would mould their characters. They not only learned physical skills like canoeing, swimming, and sailing, but they also had the experience of being with their peers, of learning to become part of a team, and of taking leadership. Ultimately, they were shaped into unique individuals with confidence, self-esteem, and acceptance of who they were.

My father's twin philosophies of recognizing and honouring one's uniqueness and of living in harmony with nature are philosophies that I grew to embrace at a very young age. My father spent his winters teaching at the university and his summers at the camp. He was the dreamer, and my mother was the driving force that made the camp dream possible. It was she who really ran things, who understood that the camp's success depended upon good planning and consistent execution of the plan. She supported his vision with her characteristic practicality, and she was largely responsible for bringing that vision to fruition.

Although I was born in Toronto, the eldest of four children, our family spent every summer together at Camp Ponacka. I had the opportunity to listen to the talks my father gave and to see the example that he set by the way he lived. I was able to see the connection he made between philosophy and real life, and that connection has anchored my world ever since.

I realize now that my father's life was shaped by his vision of what he wanted it to be. He was a visionary first and a businessman second. His approach was to focus not so much on the business aspects of running the camp as on making his vision a reality. He trusted that the resources to pursue his vision would come eventually, and they did, but not without a struggle. And my father's vision inspired him right to the very end of his life.

In 2006, Camp Ponacka celebrated its 60th anniversary. It has become a model for camps of its kind. My sister and brother-in-law have taken on the tremendous responsibility of continuing my father's vision, and they and some of their children spend their summers at the camp and continue to shape young people's lives in much the same way that my father did.

I believe that my father succeeded in living a RichLife. He eventually prospered, and he gave far more than he received. By his teaching and example my father showed me how to recognize that I had my own unique gifts - that each of us has our own talents and skills, and that each of us is valuable. I learned the importance of developing my capabilities. I learned the importance of learning to work with others. And I learned the importance of having a vision to guide my efforts and activities.

Uncle Robert's Story

My father and his Uncle Robert were a study in contrasts. Uncle Robert had left Austria for England where he became first a British citizen and then a British consul. But he eventually moved to Lugano, Switzerland, attracted by the strong Swiss currency, the more clement Swiss weather, and the beauty of Lake Lugano itself.

Uncle Robert did not grasp the concept of a RichLife. His definition of rich was determined solely by the number at the bottom of his bank statement. Uncle Robert's goal in life was to build the value of his assets into $1 million, a sizeable sum in those days. He had no vision beyond accumulating as much wealth as possible, and enough was never enough: Uncle Robert's money never made him happy. His money ruled his life, and his mood on any given day depended on the performance of the stock market.

When I first married, my husband and I went to Lugano to visit Uncle Robert. He was a bachelor, and he had become very much a creature of habit. While we were visiting, he took us to dinner at the restaurant where he had eaten dinner every night for many years, always sitting at the same table, always ordering from the same waiter. That night, because my uncle had guests with him, the waiter brought two small bottles of water to our table.

Uncle Robert became upset and complained to the waiter. He told the waiter that he should have brought one large bottle of water instead of two small ones because two small bottles cost a few cents more. At the end of our visit, Uncle Robert gave us a tea towel as a wedding gift.

My parents had a similar experience during a visit with Uncle Robert. He invited them to the same restaurant, where he ordered the daily special, just as he had always done in the past. The special did not appeal to my father, so he asked the waiter for a menu. Uncle Robert was aghast – menu items were more expensive than the special! "He focused his life on making money," said his niece, my Aunt Margit. "That was his sole purpose in life."

In the process of acquiring wealth, he never realized the satisfaction of achieving a goal, of doing good, of using his money to fuel a dream beyond the dream of more wealth. Perhaps he never allowed himself to dream. In the end, not only did he have to leave his money behind as we all do, but the legacy he left was simply the memory of his frugality – a sad contrast to my father, who was remembered fondly by hundreds of young men who had known him at Camp Ponacka, and also by grateful members of his community who appreciated his many volunteer activities.

My Story

During all the years that he was studying and teaching, my father's love of farming stayed very much alive. He had never abandoned the dream that he had put on hold when he was forced to flee his home in Czechoslovakia to save his life, and then again when he moved from his fruit farm to Toronto. It had always been part of his ideal to live in the country and be close to nature, so he gave up teaching and bought a small farm near Peterborough, Ontario.

So we moved, and I left North Toronto at the age of seven to live on a farm, leaving streets and sidewalks and an urban environment for a life in the country, near the water. I had been growing up in the city where I was used to walking to school and playing in a square patch of backyard with my friends, going to the colourful Santa Claus parade, seeing the Christmas windows at Eaton's main store on College Street. Now I had to take a bus to school, give up the backyard for the farmyard, watch the Santa Claus parade on black and white TV, and see the Christmas windows only in the Eaton's catalogue. It was a big adjustment, but on that farm I realized the affinity for nature that I had absorbed from my father. And to this day I live with a foot in both worlds – I love the pace and sophistication of urban life, and I'm equally happy getting my hands dirty in the gardens at my summer cottage.

When I graduated from high school, I enrolled in the University of Toronto even though my father did not really want me to pursue a university education. He thought the money and time would be wasted on me, because I would soon find a husband, marry, and have children, and he believed that a woman's job was to stay at home with the children. He wanted me to get my teaching certificate because he thought that I could work as a teacher until I became Mrs. Somebody.

I found this a little bizarre because my best friend's father, who was a blue-collar worker, brought her up to believe she could do anything she wanted, and he was her biggest cheerleader. Her father, who encouraged her to go to law school and become a lawyer, inspired her. But my father, the educated professor, perhaps through no fault of his own, continued to live in the same chauvinistic, old-school world in which he had grown up. It was only upon reflection much later in my life that I found inspiration from the way my father lived his life.

I took a Bachelor's degree with a major in English and French, and when I graduated my parents encouraged me take a secretarial course so that I could be "employable." Then I got married and worked in a series of jobs "suitable for women." I worked as a secretary, then moved into sales of office equipment, and just when my career was blossoming I resigned to follow my husband to his new position in Thunder Bay. Three years later my marriage ended and I found myself back in Toronto and single.

I became an entrepreneur and ran a small word processing consulting business until too-rapid technological change forced me to fold the venture. I finally found my niche when I started working in the investment industry. I worked first in institutional equity sales and then in the private client world. It was a long and circuitous path, but I now do work that I love, that I excel at, and that I think is important; I manage the financial assets of wealthy clients through advice and planning, helping them to live a rich and abundant life.

My RichLife Journey

This book is part of my RichLife journey. It was inspired by the story of my family, a family alternately rich in advantages and toughened by adversity. And it is informed by my decades of experience as a financial professional.

I've worked with many clients over the years, and they seem to fall into one of two camps: some are concerned only with their wealth and the additional wealth that it can generate, and others are concerned about enhancing their assets and ensuring that their wealth accomplishes something beyond itself. The latter exemplify RichLife balance. They do not let money become their master. Instead, they become masters of their money as they enjoy it now and direct its use toward the accomplishment of well-thought-out goals.

I used to think that any meaningful contribution I could make to life would have to take place outside my work. I could not see how managing money would allow me to make a real difference. But I now understand that my contribution to my clients can make a significant difference to their financial success.

I get to do the work that I love, have a great impact on my clients' finances and on their lives, and have a great life while doing it. I realize now that my work is the vehicle that helps me live well, give back while I'm here, and leave a legacy for when I'm gone – and through my work, I can help my clients to do the same.

The best contribution I can make is to help people create clarity, confidence, and peace of mind about their finances. As my coach, Dan Sullivan of The Strategic Coach® (a business program for entrepreneurs) says, "The role of being a good financial advisor is to provide leadership, relationship, and creativity." My journey has taught me to exercise leadership by making sure that my clients know not only about their money but also about what they can achieve with their money. My relationship with my clients includes getting to know them as people, earning their trust in the knowledge and dedication of me and my team, and providing them with peace of mind about their finances. My creativity involves understanding their financial goals, and then finding and using the right products and services to meet those goals.

I started this chapter with a story about my father's life, and now I think it is fitting to end it by sharing a gift my daughter Sarah gave to me. She used to recite a poem every day at summer camp, and she loved it so much that she taught it to me. It has now become one of my favourite poems, and it expresses succinctly the spirit in which I approached the writing of this book, the spirit of the RichLife.

Salutation to the Dawn

Kalidasa, Hindu Poet and Dramatist

Look to this day!

For it is life, the very life of life.

In its brief course

Lie all the verities and realities of your existence:

The bliss of growth;

The glory of action;

The splendour of achievement;

For yesterday is but a dream,

And tomorrow is only a vision,

But today, well lived, makes every

Yesterday

A dream of happiness

And every tomorrow a vision of hope.

Look well, therefore, to this day!

Such is the salutation to the dawn.

Chapter 2

THE RICHLIFE: PROSPERITY WITH PASSION AND PURPOSE

> **rich** *adjective* 1. having much wealth. 2. …splendid, costly, elaborate. 3. valuable. 4 copious, abundant, ample. 5. abundantly supplied with… 8. mellow and deep, strong and full.
> *Canadian Oxford Dictionary, Second Edition*

It seems that the word "rich" is associated today more with money and splendour and less with abundance, depth, and fullness. But when I talk about the RichLife, "rich" has both connotations.

After more than twenty years of helping clients to manage and grow their assets, I have discovered that the place of money in a person's life indicates a lot about how they live their life. As a financial advisor, my role is to preserve the wealth my clients have accumulated and to increase it over time. And the way people have acquired their money is as varied as the people themselves.

Some of my clients earned their money by realizing entrepreneurial dreams – starting a business, investing their lives in it, and having the business thrive. Their businesses provided a comfortable living, and when they finally sold their business assets, they received a significant sum that needed to be invested and protected. Other people have inherited their money. Still others have received money through divorce. Many people have simply earned their money through their careers or professions.

What interests me is the story behind the wealth. When I talk to my clients, what I hear behind their conversation about their assets are stories of vision and risk. Challenge, failure, and victory. Passion and commitment. Disappointment. Apprehension. Celebration.

So when I talk about a RichLife, I'm not referring only to the numbers that define wealth. When I think of a RichLife, I think of what it took for people to get to where they are, what kind of lives they are living now, and what kind of future they will have. I think of what they will leave behind to nurture and inspire others.

Money and the Art of Living Well

It is a curious thing that people often leave money out of their answer when asked, "How do you define the art of living?" Members of the well-known musical group The Canadian Brass, who have made the brass quintet a vehicle for serious concert music and who have more than 60 recordings to their credit, gave answers such as "blending your dedication to your professional goal with your dedication to family," "a balance of exciting peaks and down times," "honing the ability to enjoy two things at once: the spiritual aspect…and our lives as people in the everyday world," and "There are only two deathbed questions for me, and they are: 'Did you learn?' And, 'Did you love well?'" (*Stir Magazine*, February 2005)

And in his book *Infinite Life: The Seven Virtues for Living Well*, Robert Thurman listed these virtues as: wisdom, generosity, justice, patience, creativity, contemplation, and the art of infinite living.

So, obviously, living well does not necessarily mean having a lot of money. However, the challenge for the wealthy is to define living well in the context of their affluence, but not solely as their affluence.

What's your definition? What does living the RichLife mean for you? What will it take for you to look back at your life with a sense of satisfaction and fulfillment? I have heard some sad stories from my clients through the years, and each time I hear one it makes me wish that I could have met this person years earlier and helped them see that their finances are an important part of their life, but not their whole life.

I think it is instructive to consider how money figures in the grand scheme of some real people's lives. Some seem to have figured out early what living well means in a RichLife context, how to let their money drive their vision. Others never seem to get beyond their money to develop a fuller vision of what their lives could be.

As an example of someone who figured it out early, consider David Loch. David is an art consultant, collector, and gallery owner with galleries in Toronto, Winnipeg, and Calgary. The motto of the Loch Gallery is "Let art enrich your life." For David, the question "What is life without art?" is more than merely rhetorical. He is passionate about art. He equates living a RichLife with having art in his life, and he really believes that art can enrich everyone's life. He has a passion for making a difference, and art is the tool he uses to make that difference – in the lives of both the artists and the many people who might never see this art without his commitment.

David loves to foster emerging artists, much as my grandmother did back in Prague all those many years ago. He has made a huge impact on the art world by identifying talented Canadian artists and promoting their works. He has brought them out of their quiet studios and into the mainstream art world where many have received public recognition of their work. He is able to do this because he knows good art and he knows wealthy patrons who are interested in supporting the talents of up-and-coming artists.

David recently held an event to showcase the work of several artists, and each of them spoke about where and how they find the source of their creative inspiration. The artists and patrons then sat down to lunch together to continue the discussion more informally, and to get to know one another more personally. This is the kind of connection that David makes possible through his work.

As it turns out, some of the artists were a bit surprised to find how much enjoyment others derived from their paintings – they had always tended to create for themselves, and the discovery that others really understood and appreciated their work was a huge gift for them. Another gift is the fact that with broader recognition comes more demand for their art, and that means money that allows them to spend more time creating. The Loch Gallery story is an excellent example of a RichLife that is *enabled* by money rather than *defined* by money.

In contrast to David, let us look at someone who has never been able to develop a clear perspective on what is really important to him. Some of my clients come to me because they find themselves suddenly wealthy and have no experience managing a large sum of money. Mr. Jameson (not his real name), who had acquired his wealth through the sale of his hardware distribution business to a US conglomerate, is a case in point. At our first meeting, he told me that he had had a heart attack a few years before, and that even with that "wake-up call" he had kept at his business with his usual vigour. Even now, although he has sold the business, he is working just as hard managing it for the parent company.

With his newly liquid wealth, he built a three-million-dollar house, but once it was finished, he decided he did not really like it, and so he put it on the market. As he spoke about the house, he also told me stories about a family cottage where he had spent much of his childhood, and he talked about how much he had loved the time he spent there. The cottage was now abandoned and in serious disrepair, but he did not have the time or the inclination to use some of his new wealth to refurbish it.

As I do with all new clients, I asked him what would have to happen for him to look back at the end of his life and feel that he had no regrets. I could tell that it was a novel question to him: he was visibly taken aback. He said something indecipherable about his four children, and he mentioned again how busy he was managing the company. I asked him to think about my question and to give me an answer at our next meeting, but he was reluctant to do even that. He said, "I'm too busy to find an answer."

He was too busy with bigger issues such as selling the house and managing the company. He just did not have time to think about anything but "practical" questions. And although his wife told me that he had talked about retiring and spending time travelling, she thought the idea frightened him. She said that his identity was so fully wrapped up in his work that the questions of who he would be, what he would do, and how he could be useful outside the context of work were too upsetting for him to think about.

In the end, he never did answer my question. He had not created anything greater with his wealth, he was not really sure what he wanted to do with it, and he had vague but unarticulated regrets about his choices. He had finally amassed a great deal of money, but it brought him no enduring satisfaction. Instead, it bought him a big house he did not even like. And in the meantime, his completely work-focused life had eroded his health and his family relationships. His was definitely not the RichLife.

The story of the Marshalls (not their real name) is similar. They too had worked hard throughout their lives and had managed to build a thriving business. They too sold their business and were reeling a bit with the realization that their sizeable net worth was no longer tied up in real estate and inventory – it was now completely liquid, and they were terrified at the challenge of managing it. They did not stay on as managers of the business, but neither were they able to relax into the comfort of financial security.

The Marshalls had always been hoarders. A visit to their home showed the degree to which they needed to hold onto what they had. Their house was so full of things – furniture inherited from elderly relatives, items that had not been discarded when they were replaced with newer pieces, books and papers – that the couple lived in just two rooms, the only rooms with space to live. On the weekends they would escape to their cottage, which was not nearly so crowded.

With the sale of their business, the Marshalls' lives became complicated with worry about their new-found wealth. Driven by a fear of being victimized, resentful of the taxes they would have to pay, and frustrated by the requests for money from a variety of sources, they constantly fretted about their money, and they transferred their habit of hoarding to their money as well. In fact, even though Mrs. Marshall suffered from severe arthritis and also developed cancer, they would not spend a few dollars for the comfort of a cab ride and instead continued to walk the 10 blocks or so to my office for meetings.

They were so intent on holding on to all their money that they could not see some of the obvious good they could have done with it. For instance, they never considered gifting – or even lending – any of their money to their three adult daughters, even though such a gift could have made an enormous difference to each of them: one was a single mother struggling to provide for herself and her child, one needed funds to pursue further education, and the husband of the third daughter had been laid off from work and was having trouble finding gainful employment. Unfortunately, the only benefit that the children would receive from the money would be delayed until they inherited it.

The Marshalls did talk about building a new house, but they could not agree on the type of house or even on its location, and so this dream never materialized. The

Marshalls never realized that their money could buy choice and change and new beginnings as they entered their retirement years. Like Mr. Jameson, they simply did not grasp the concept of how to live a RichLife.

The Poor Man's Syndrome

How much money is enough? It is an interesting question. Try it out at a family barbecue – I bet you'll stir the pot! However we define *enough*, we never really reach enough until we begin to give away some of what we have. It's as if we think, "If I have enough to share, then I must have enough."

People like my father's uncle who accumulate a lot of money often get trapped in the poor man's syndrome: what they have is never enough, they always want more. These people live with a scarcity mentality. On the other hand, people who give money away live with an abundance mentality; they tend to be optimistic about their circumstances and trust that the future will be at least as good as the present. And many find that their giving results in a renewed sense of purpose and meaning.

"A lack of meaning is more detrimental to life satisfaction than stress and worries." (Ulrich Schimmack, Professor of Psychology, University of Toronto)

Getting to the Source of the RichLife

When I think of delivering my father's eulogy, I am thankful for the revelations that came to me that day. I have thought a lot since then about what makes a RichLife, and if I can borrow a phrase from Carolyn Richardson Hursh (chairman of the board of James Richardson & Sons Ltd., and a trained social worker, philanthropist, and business leader), a RichLife consists of "learning, earning, and returning."

Just as every person's story is different, every person's passion is different. And as a financial advisor, I need to understand my clients' passions in order to align their investments with their lives. When I meet a new client, I always ask the same two questions.

I learned the basis for these questions through my association with Dan Sullivan of The Strategic Coach®. He asks a question that he calls The R-Factor Question®, where R stands for Relationship. The R-Factor Question® has a three-year time frame. I have modified the question to be applicable to an entire lifetime.* I use both the The R-Factor Question® and the modified R-Factor Question® with my clients. If my clients are willing to answer these questions thoughtfully, I am assured that we can build a mutually beneficial relationship through which I can help them meet their goals.

I begin with the modified R-Factor Question®. "What has to happen for you to feel you've lived your life with no regrets?" This is a question that demands a long-term perspective, and it often takes my clients by surprise. Many have been so focused on the daily task of running a business, accumulating wealth, and managing their wealth that they

* The R-Factor Question is a registered trademark, protected by copyright and integral concept of The Strategic Coach, Inc. All rights reserved. Used and modified with written permission. www.strategiccoach.com

have forgotten the passion and the vision that were their initial inspiration.

The question prompts people to step outside the arena of their everyday concerns and affords them an opportunity for self-examination that they may not have allowed themselves in a long time. They get permission to ask themselves, "If money were no object…" My question always helps them to focus on purpose, to recall – or redefine – their vision and their passion; it lets them put their financial concerns on temporary hold. For many, this question prompts the realization that their money is not an end in itself, but a means to achieving other ends that are important to them.

My second question is the R-Factor Question®: "Three years from now, what would have to have happened for you to look back and be happy about your progress?" A three-year time horizon helps people focus on relatively immediate concerns. The answer usually has to do with getting organized, accomplishing something, reaching or passing a significant life event, getting affairs sorted out. If the lifetime question is a question about being, the three-year question is really more a question about doing.

I ask the lifetime question first because "if you don't know where you're going, any path will take you there." (paraphrased from Lewis Carroll's *Alice in Wonderland*) This question focuses on vision and passion. Then the three-year question focuses more on "How do I start to get there from here?" In between these two questions is the life that connects them.

Many people have not really thought about what connects their present to their vision of the future. Some of my clients choose not to answer the R-Factor Questions immediately; they prefer to take them home and think about them for a while. The questions spark reflection, and many clients say that they have sparked conversations with spouses and other family members about what is really important. Some couples have told me that talking over the answers to these questions has even caused recommitment and rejuvenation of their relationships.

When I meet with clients again after they have thought over these questions, they usually have a much better sense of where they are going and what they would like to do with their money. Then I can help them invest, and yes, sometimes even spend.

I have had clients react with surprise when I encourage them to spend some of their money or when I applaud them for having done so. They know that my foremost responsibility as a financial advisor is to preserve and enhance their wealth. And certainly the more money they have for me to manage, the more money I earn for my work. But I also consider it a responsibility to my clients to get them to think about the intangible returns of spending some of their money. They often come to realize that money well spent in the present has both immediate and ongoing rewards, and that these rewards can be every bit as important in their own way as the returns that could be generated on the money if it were invested instead of spent.

I have a client named John Smith who has a cottage on an island, and he had a boat that was both old and out of repair. He really needed and wanted a new boat, but he could not give himself permission to buy one. I knew his financial position and his lifestyle, and I knew he could well afford the cost of a new boat. We sat down and reviewed his finances together, and I said, "You can spend this money and you will still have enough." That is all he needed to hear. Our review gave him confidence in his financial situation, and he felt like he had permission to buy the boat.

In the grand scheme of things, it was a slight expenditure, but it had a big impact on his enjoyment of his cottage time. Other clients already know they can spend the money, yet they still ask, and I still tell them, "Yes! Take that trip. Do that family reunion."

The RichLife Mantra: Live Well, Give Back, Leave a Legacy

I have been using The R-Factor Questions for a long time to help people think about their money and what it means to them in the broader context of their lives. I have heard many different answers to these questions, but if there is one lesson that remains with me, it is this:

Having a RichLife is not just about money. It is not just about investments in stocks and bonds. Having a RichLife is also about living well. It is about giving back. It is about leaving a legacy. It is about money, certainly, but it is also about investment in life, in people, in the future.

Live Well. What image immediately comes to mind when you read these words? What does living well look like for you? Does it mean that you are active, engaged, alert, spirited?

Does it mean you have the things that money can buy? A beautiful home, and perhaps a second home in cottage country or in a warm climate? A comfortable car, good meals, season tickets to the opera or to the ball game?

Or does it mean you have the things that money cannot necessarily buy but that money certainly enables? Things like health and wellness. Continuous learning. Freedom to choose your activities when you want and where you want.

Does living well mean having meaningful work? Work that gives you a sense of fulfillment and satisfaction, work that you see not just as a way to make a living but as a way to make a difference?

Does living well mean that your life is rich with meaningful relationships? Do you have friends who are kindred spirits? Do you have the ability to be with them whenever you choose, or whenever they need you? Does living well mean that your family members not only speak to you, but they also speak to each other? I say this tongue in cheek, but I have seen the strife that financial discussions can create among family members. For many, a happy home life is essential to their sense of living well.

There are probably as many images of what it means to live well as there are people in the world, but there is a recurring theme when my clients talk to me about what it means to them. Living well always seems to be about realizing the benefit of what they spend their time doing, about reaping what they have sown. It is about giving themselves permission to enjoy what they have created, now, in the moment, before the opportunity passes.

Give Back. Toss a pebble in the lake and watch the ripples reach the far shore. The ripple effect shows the ongoing results of one simple toss, and it is an apt metaphor for giving back - because what someone gives back now can have a huge impact both now and in the future.

Wealthy people are in a unique position to make a substantial contribution to their communities, to their favourite charitable causes, to their own families. And for many, giving back is almost second nature. They appreciate their privileged position and they accept that it brings with it certain responsibilities. But for some, the reward of giving back is not just the feeling of having fulfilled a responsibility, it is the pleasure of knowing that they have been able to make a difference.

But when it comes to family, it is not always easy to know how much of a difference to make in your children's lives. I have seen sons and daughters who never seem to find their own direction in life because their parents give them money when it would be better to withhold it. On the other hand, I have also seen sons and daughters whose lives are full of needless hardship simply because their parents hold back support. An article in the *Bay Street Bull* (February 2006) reported that "the highest status symbol among the affluent is adult children who are self-supporting." Perhaps Warren Buffett put it best when he suggested that parents should give their children enough that they can do anything they want, but not so much that they can do nothing.

Leave a Legacy. Giving back is for when you are here. Leaving a legacy is for when you are gone. It is not really about the money, it is about what can be done with it after you no longer have any earthly use for it. And it is also about how you will you be remembered.

Many secondary schools engage their students in an exercise of writing their own eulogy, or their obituary, or the epitaph that will be written on the headstone at their grave. It is an exercise that makes them think about how they want to be remembered. Then they are encouraged to live up to the picture of how they wish to be remembered. Some of us would no doubt benefit from such an exercise.

People live on in the memories of their children and grandchildren because they touch their lives in such an intimate way. My daughter was given a book entitled *Mom, Share Your Life With Me* by Kathy Lashier. The book starts with the first day of a mother's life, and asks question after question. Do you have a good piece of advice for me? Tell of the closest friend you had during childhood. Tell about a big fib you told. Questions and answers. And so much more than that, because the telling of stories is the creation of memories. It is the richness that comes from shared history. It is the instilling of values, and the lessons learned from triumphs and regrets. If we had not had these questions, I might never have come to share myself in this way with my daughter.

I am not sure anyone wants to be remembered simply for how much money they left behind; I think they would rather be remembered for some greater purpose that their money accomplished. What legacy will you leave? Will the money you leave be used in the way you hope it will? Are you planning now to ensure that it will be? And what do you want your legacy to be about aside from the value of your estate?

What Is A RichLife?

For David Loch, a RichLife is a life filled with art.

For someone with a passion for nature, a RichLife is enjoying and helping to preserve the environment.

For parents, a RichLife may be knowing that their children love and respect one another, and that they will be friends long after the parents are no longer around.

For some, a RichLife may be having the wisdom and knowledge that come from personal experience, and it may be sharing that wisdom and knowledge.

For the affluent, a RichLife may mean comfort that their assets are adequately protected and satisfaction in knowing that their wealth allows them to make a tangible contribution.

Purpose. Future. Dreams. Family. Money. Goals. Freedom. Charity. Meaning. Community. Happiness.

Achievement. Any or all of these may be elements of your RichLlife. But whatever your definition of a RichLife, there is joy to be found in discovering what your life can be and what it can mean if you are really intentional about it.

Chapter 3

MAKING MONEY… AND MAKING YOUR MONEY MATTER

"Wealth is not his that has it, but his that enjoys it." Benjamin Franklin

As a child I remember hearing Doris Day sing the famous song *Que Sera, Sera* with its lyrics about a fate that is simply delivered to us.

Living a RichLife is about the choices we make. We choose to live well. We choose to give back. We choose to leave a legacy. We choose our attitude. We choose to be happy.

So, even though I loved Doris Day's song, life is not really about what will be no matter what, it is more about what we choose. But I wonder how many of us go through life numb to the possibility that we can choose our future.

Viktor Frankl, the noted psychiatrist and author who escaped death in the Nazi concentration camps, observed that "Everything can be taken from a man but…the last of the human freedoms – to choose one's attitude in any given set of circumstances, to choose one's own way."

The bookstores are filled with self-help books that promote the six steps to this and the seven rules of that, all committed to help us reach some level of happiness. And just as the definition of a RichLife is as unique as the individual defining it, the definition of happiness is equally as individual.

It has been said that money cannot buy happiness. Yet we spend so much of our energy today pursuing money, hoping that when we have enough, we'll be happy. But we have already seen how difficult it can be to decide how much is enough. For many, it seems to have something to do with how much other people have. We seem to measure our wealth and success in relation to others, to what they have and what they buy. It sometimes seems that numbers alone define wealth. Yet we have agreed that the source of the RichLife is not always found in a person's bank account.

In the RichLife, money is an enabler. It can be the means by which we reach a goal or realize a dream. Money gives us choice; it gives us the opportunity to live well.

Consider, for instance, the story of my friend Cathy. When she was diagnosed with cancer, she could not obtain in Canada the resources and medical technology she needed to save her life – they simply weren't available here. Fortunately, she had the financial resources to travel to a non-traditional medical clinic in the United States where she could find and pay for the expensive treatment that has extended her life. If she had stayed in Canada she would have died. Instead she is living a longer life because she could afford the help she needed.

Money can be used to save a life, and it can be used to make a life fuller. Take travel, for example. I recently travelled to the Galapagos Islands with my daughter. The trip gave us some very special time together learning about this unspoiled part of the world. We could imagine that it remains today much as it was when it inspired Charles Darwin. Our trip will be a wonderful lifelong memory for both of us. The money allowed us to make a choice about what we wanted to do together. Our choice was about sharing an experience. For others it could be a matter of life and death, as it was for Cathy.

And sometimes it takes living without much money to understand the place you want money to have in your life. My nephew studied business in university, and when he graduated, he was not sure what he wanted to do. He used an inheritance of $5,000 to move to Mexico for six months. He had to be frugal to make the money last, and he now realizes that although he can "live poor," he does not really want to. This experience motivated him to think seriously about lifestyle and what he wants to do with his life, knowing that he is the one responsible for the way he lives.

Choice and Consequences

In the RichLife, money is important partly because of the control it gives us over our lives. On his website at http://www.coachjim.com, professional life coach, speaker, and author Jim M. Allen listed ten things that are under a person's control. They are:

- What you say
- What you think
- What you do
- Your work
- Who you associate with
- Your health
- The environment you live in

- Your finances
- Your time
- Your legacy

Of these ten, eight are directly affected by your financial situation.

What you say and what you think are both linked to your internal conversations, to your attitude toward life and your sense of purpose. As such, they are not directly influenced by how much money you have. But your financial situation directly affects the other eight items on the list in many ways.

Suffice it to say that what you do in your life is a matter of making choices about activities, and the amount of money you have either broadens or restricts the choices you are able to make. It helps determine whether you work or not, what kind of work you do, the leisure activities you engage in, the level of health care you are able to provide for yourself and your family, where you live, and the way you choose to spend your time.

Obviously, your financial health is dependent upon your finances. That is, if you have just enough money to meet your monthly obligations, where is the money going to come from for investment in your future?

The legacy you leave is not simply how much money you have, but how you plan for what you want your assets to accomplish after you die. Again, the choices are almost innumerable. It could be a charitable donation that means your money will continue to do good, and it may even get your name on a plaque, on a scholarship, or on the wall of a hospital wing. It could be leaving your children financially secure. Or it could be covering the cost of your grandchildren's post-secondary education, and perhaps graduate school, at the institution of their choice. Or perhaps devising a plan that will allow all your grandchildren and their children to continue to enjoy the family cottage. Or simply planning thoughtfully so that your children will not become divided from one another as they divide your estate among themselves.

In the RichLife, money smoothes out the roughness of the road, but it is not the destination. It is important because it broadens the choices we can make about our lives, and because it enables us to act on those choices.

Fear and Excitement

As a financial advisor to my clients, I want to ensure that their financial affairs are structured in a way that protects and enhances the value of their assets. As a trusted advisor, I also want my clients to live a RichLife now – to Live Well, to Give Back, and to plan to Leave a Legacy that lasts beyond the next generation. I want my clients to look back on their lives without regret.

I often ask my clients, "What wakes you up in the middle of the night?" I want to know what is so significant that it stays active in their subconscious, creating excitement and anticipation or fostering fear and regret. I ask them this because I know that the answer will help me understand them and what is important to them.

Their answers are varied, but there are certain themes that keep coming up, both positive and negative: excitement and anticipation, fear and greed, relief and thankfulness, worry and regret, suspicion and judgment. Here are some examples of what clients have told me:

- I'm about to sell my company, and I can hardly believe the sense of freedom and excitement I feel.
- I don't know what to do with my money. I'm afraid someone will take advantage of me.
- This is my last chance to acquire sufficient wealth to last until I die. I'm worried that the money I've accumulated may not keep me in the same lifestyle when I retire.
- My daughter is getting married in six months, and I'm waking up with all kinds of ideas for her wedding.
- I am getting a lot of free advice about what to do with my money and it all involves making someone else rich.
- I need a game plan for my money. I want to maximize my return.
- I've got a tremendous opportunity to expand my business internationally, and new details of my strategy keep coming to me between three and five in the morning.
- My husband and I can't agree on how to spend our money. We don't want the same things.
- My kids are already beginning to squabble over who gets what. I'm worried that they won't remain friends when I'm gone.

Whatever their response, when my clients answer this question, they are allowing me a glimpse into important current concerns in their lives. And whether their responses are positive or negative, once I know what their concerns are, I also know how I can help them sort out their issues, create order and structure in their affairs.

Scotch on the Rocks, Marriage on the Rocks

I had a friend who really knew how to live well. Sheila MacRandal had been diagnosed with cancer, and even though she was dying she was living with hope. She carried on in the best state of normalcy that she could muster. In spite of the undignified nature of her cancer treatment, she kept her spirits high. She refused to give up hope and cave into this terrible disease. She continued to make plans and to talk about the future. All her talk was about being alive – there was no talk of dying.

She had an adorable little cottage that was called *Scotch on the Rocks.* It was perched high on a cliff above a beautiful lake, and she spent a lot of time there in the summers. When she was ill, I used to take her muffins and soups, and one day she invited me to visit her at her cottage. When I arrived, she had a beautiful table set out on the deck with pastries and juice – she had gone all out to entertain me. I knew she was sick, but I did not know how sick she really was.

As we sat and enjoyed the summer weather, I admired the lake and her cottage, and she began to talk about what next summer would hold for her. She planned to paint the front door before then. As she spoke, I said to myself, "She's not going to be here next summer." Sure enough, in October she died, and she never did see that front door painted. But her spirit, her "never-give-up" attitude, kept her dreams and her fantasies alive until the very last minute.

She made the best of her time and never forgot how to have a laugh. Her spirit was an inspiration for everyone around her. Her spirit and her sense of humour helped her and us to handle everything, and that was part of the legacy she left. That was part of her RichLife.

It is too bad that not everyone can live with Sheila's understanding of what is important in life. One of my clients was a senior executive with a Fortune 500 company. He developed an international reputation and spent a lot of time travelling overseas. Alan Hudson was so focused on his career that he did not notice what was happening to his home life until it was too late. Just as his tenure with the organization was coming to an end, his wife announced that she was leaving – she did not want to be with him anymore.

It took this shock for Alan to realize that he had not paid attention to the balance, or the lack of balance, in his life. He was so focused and so single-minded about his work that he had not included his wife in his activities in any meaningful way. They had grown increasingly apart, living on two different tracks, until finally they were strangers living in the same house.

He says now that he should have invested as much energy in his marriage as he did in his work. Instead, he took his wife for granted, and now he feels lost. He was rich, but he did not enjoy a RichLife.

It is said that we are remembered by our obituary, not by our resumé. I was reading *The Globe and Mail* one day when a picture of a beautiful woman with a warm and loving smile caught my eye. It was on the obituary page, and under the picture these words were written:

> "A mother that every mother should emulate, a teacher that every student should have, a performer every audience should see, the friend that every friend should be. Peacefully at age 45 after a determined and courageous battle with cancer. After a lifetime of lighting up this world with her divine voice, unique style, sparkling personality and contagious laughter. She taught us all the nature of a good heart and unconditional love. The lessons continued until the end, where we learned about dignity in the face of great suffering…Diane left her legacy. She always wanted her family to love each other." (Obituary of Diane Lewarne Partin. Reprinted from *The Globe and Mail,* December 2, 2004)

Do you think this woman lived a RichLife? I am sure of it.

Chapter 4

LIVING WELL

Pierre Berton, the famous writer and certainly one of Canada's foremost journalists, embodied the RichLife principles of Live Well, Give Back, and Leave a Legacy. Berton grew up in Dawson City, Yukon, and went to study journalism at the University of British Columbia, following his lifelong dream of becoming a journalist.

In addition to his journalistic achivements in the print and electronic media, Berton also turned his considerable writing talent to the chronicling of Canadian history. He made Canada's history come alive in a way that no one else has, and his books are read and studied by many who want to understand our country better.

Pierre Berton was used to the northern way of life, and he chose not to live in Toronto even though he worked there. He moved to the small village of Kleinburg, Ontario, with its rutted dirt roads and more rugged lifestyle. He made the trip to Toronto every day, long before this type of commuting became common practice. Although he and his wife may not literally have been pioneers in Kleinburg, they loved the village and were instrumental in preserving its historical heritage.

As the village expanded to a town and then became part of the suburbs of the city, Berton and his wife focused on keeping the original village and its main street intact, authentic, traditional. Berton's commitment to live well in an environment that he loved led him to give back to the community by preserving its heritage, and this work created a huge part of the Berton legacy. There is talk now of making a Pierre Berton museum in Kleinburg. There is certainly enough memorabilia of his life to create a fascinating museum, and it would be a fitting way to honour the impact of his work.

Pierre Berton also created an environment in which others can experience their RichLife. Writers need peace and quiet and freedom from distractions in order to pursue their art. Berton knew this, and he thought the Yukon was the perfect place for writers to get away from it all, to escape the pressure of having to work at paid employment while they wrote. So he bought the Dawson City house he had grown up in and turned it into a writers' retreat.

Through the Writers Retreat Society, he raised money to help fund the activities of Berton House. The writers who come to Berton House are not working to a deadline. They are encouraged and nurtured and provided with a place of retreat where they can develop their art. In return, they agree to interact with the local community and media. Many writers who have spent time at Berton House talk about what a positive experience it was to live and work in that environment and to know that they were implicitly trusted to use their time there in a constructive and meaningful way.

Along with Margaret Laurence, David Young, Margaret Atwood, and Graeme Gibson, Berton also established The Writers' Development Trust (now known as The Writers' Trust of Canada). This organization provides awards to writers and sponsors events to raise money and awareness of literature and literacy.

Berton chose to live according to his passions – writing and history. He lived in a way that served him well and that served others well, too. He gave back to the community of Kleinburg and to the broader community of Canadian writers while he was living and able to see how his efforts could provide what they wanted and needed. And when he died he left a rich legacy – his town, his memories, and his significant chronicling of the history of his beloved country, Canada. His was truly a RichLife.

Your Life is in Your Hands

Take another look at this book's cover illustration. Three smooth, rounded river stones in open hands – each stone engraved with the words of the RichLife mantra. Live Well. Give Back. Leave a Legacy.

Choosing to Live Well means choosing your values, understanding what is important to you, and recognizing the priorities that will maintain balance in your life.

Many of today's wealthy people lived through the war years when they were focused on survival, when they worked hard just to put food on the table and clothing on their children. But we are now in an era of unprecedented prosperity. We are also at a point at which a great deal of the existing wealth is destined to go from the hands of those who acquired it into the hands of their children and grandchildren, or into philanthropic work.

Today there is so much affluence – but there are only so many cars you can drive and so many clothes you can wear, and the material things that you acquire cannot on their own ensure you lead a RichLife or leave a RichLife legacy.

Of course, not everyone is prosperous, and those who are not can certainly lead lives that are rich in relationships and rich in meaning. But wealth creates its own opportunities for – and its own impediments to – leading a RichLife.

Some affluent people have spent their whole lives focusing on their work, and now as they reach a certain age and pause to reflect in a different way about their lives, they may find that they have lost touch with what is meaningful in their lives. Others are future-oriented as they make plans for the transfer of their wealth to the younger generations, and they want their wealth to make a difference now. It is part of what living well means to them.

Having planned for their own comfort in late adulthood, and having provided for their families, some of my clients need more than a little encouragement to enjoy the fruits of their labours now. Many have become so accustomed to a life of frugality and delayed gratification that they are reluctant to spend money on activities they could enjoy today. It could be something as simple as buying more than one pair of glasses so they can have one pair in the house, one pair at work, and one pair in their pocket, but some think it an extravagance to have so many pairs of glasses that there is always one within arm's reach. Others will not dare to take the luxury of travelling to places they have dreamed of seeing all their lives – the South Pacific, Australia, or like me, the Galapagos Islands – even though they can well afford to do so.

Many of my clients are fit and active, but others seem to need a nudge to spend money on maintaining the kind of healthy lifestyle that is so important to living well – especially in the maturing years. I encourage them to invest in their well-being by adopting a fitness and healthy eating plan. Many health clubs offer both exercise and nutrition programs.

Regular massage or yoga classes – and spa treatments – can ease both the physical and emotional impacts of stress. Regular medical assessments and alternative medical therapies can help enhance overall health and well-being. I try to show my clients that an investment in their physical well-being now will continue to pay regular dividends for the rest of their lives.

But it is not only their physical being they need to look after. Intellectual growth is just as significant in maintaining life balance and stimulating creativity and productivity. And there are lots of ways to get intellectual stimulation. Reading, seeing films, going to the theatre, attending lectures – these are all ways of keeping the mind active and engaged.

There are forums that are specifically dedicated to intellectual development and creativity. For example, since 2000, Toronto has had an annual spring gathering called *ideaCity* where people from all walks of life, from different backgrounds and with different experiences of the world, meet to talk and exchange ideas. Without the use of visual aids, people lead seminars and discussions on what makes them think, what stimulates them, what curious questions they are seeking answers for. No resolution is expected, just the spark of ideas that stimulate and synergize.

People living the RichLife do this same sort of thing every day – they live well by engaging with their world, being curious, and keeping their minds open to the possibilities that life presents.

Values: the Foundation of the RichLife

The RichLife is based on personal values. When I was an investment advisor in institutional equity sales with Merrill Lynch, part of my job was to connect professional investors with market analysts and strategists. At that time, I had no children and I was able to focus all my energies on my career, and I happily spent the long hours at work that the position demanded. Then my son Nicholas was born.

One day he had a doctor's appointment, and although I thought it might be difficult to get away from the office to take him to the doctor, I expected I would be able to do so. But I could not. And that crystallized for me how important it is for me to have control over my time. I left Merrill Lynch soon after that, and using the financial expertise I had developed, established myself as an advisor in the private client world. I have been helping individuals and their families manage their assets ever since.

I have the same work ethic and I still work hard, but now my career affords me the flexibility to take time for things that matter to me personally. It suits me better, it makes for a better fit with my family, and it provides a comfortable living.

Recently my three siblings and I were together and observed that we all make our livings by what we create or produce rather than as someone else's employees. We rely on our own smarts and hard work, and we have built great lives. We have not all necessarily accumulated lots of money, but we all have pride of ownership and the flexibility we need to pursue what is important to us. We are living well because we are living according to our values.

What are your values? What is important to you? What would you choose not to sacrifice, even if it meant a drastic change in circumstance? Where are you not willing to compromise?

The RichLife Pie

Below is a graphic representation of the five elements of health that combine to make someone's life a RichLife.

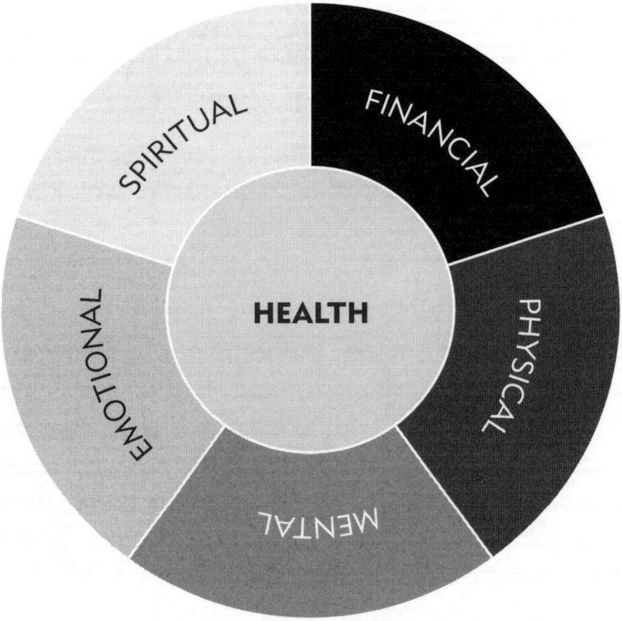

This model represents important aspects of a full and healthy life, and each is important to living well.

If you enjoy physical health, you are strong, fit, active, and productive, at work and at play.

If you enjoy mental health, you are continually learning and growing; you have a positive, optimistic outlook; and you seek out challenge and opportunity.

If you enjoy emotional health, you have a strong support network of family and friends. You contribute to their well-being as they contribute to yours. You have self-esteem and confidence in your abilities. You are proud of your contributions.

If you enjoy financial health, you have discretionary income that you can direct in the manner you choose. You may even be financially independent. You have security. Your future and your legacy are assured.

If you enjoy spiritual health, you have a sense of purpose in your life and a worldview that serves you well.

Living Healthy

There are so many aspects to health – physical, mental, emotional, financial, spiritual – and all of them are important to finding your RichLife balance. Let us take just a minute to consider emotional health. Dr. Ed Diener, Professor of Psychology at the University of Illinois, Urbana-Champaign, is often referenced for his research, which concludes that "emotional well-being is determined most significantly not by your bank account but by the quality of your social relationships and satisfaction at your work." (*Scarlett Magazine*, Dec./Jan. 2005)

Here is an example of how two of my clients live well by supporting the emotional well-being of their employees. John and Dian Bell have a company that manufactures auto parts. Dian took me on a tour of their plant and introduced me to some of the staff running the machinery.

Some employees were eager to explain what they were doing and how they were doing it. Some had photos of the finished car that their particular part would go into, and they referred to the photos as they spoke. They explained where the part they were making would go in the vehicle and showed me what it would look like when it was finished. They were obviously very connected to what they were doing.

Interestingly though, some of the employees did not know which vehicle the parts they were making would be used in. They seemed content simply to come to the plant, do their work, take their coffee breaks, and then go home.

Dian and John had realized long ago that they needed to help their employees feel connected to their work and valued for a job well done. And so they had established an employee recognition program to accomplish this. Their program connected recognition with aspects of the RichLife such as emotional health and physical well-being – the rewards included memberships at the YMCA/YWCA to serve the recreational needs of the employees and their families.

John and Dian's employee recognition program is doubly effective: it contributes to the emotional well-being of their employees by helping them enhance their pride and satisfaction in their work, and it contributes to their physical well-being by providing the facilities for healthy recreation. Some employees respond, others do not, but certainly John and Dian's idea of living well includes helping others to do so. And that is definitely a RichLife attitude.

Making Connections

Much of living well has to do with our many different connections and the contributions they make to our lives. One day I took a blank piece of paper and listed all my clients, friends and acquaintances, and then I drew connecting lines between those who knew each other. It was quite interesting to see how one person had led me to another, and then that one to yet another. Sometimes one person had initiated a whole chain of connections.

As many people do, I have friends from all walks of life, and of course not all of them know each other. Years ago, though, I was thinking about the fact that I would often talk to friends about one another, and it occurred to me that it would be fun to get them all together.

So in 1983 I invited a group of women friends to my cottage for a weekend getaway – friends from high school, friends from the squash team at the Elmwood Club, friends that I had met through work. Every one of them accepted my invitation. We now call our group "Women in the Wilderness," and we have been getting together regularly ever since.

Out of those gatherings people have formed friendships that have nothing to do with me except that I introduced them. Now, 23 years later, the core group is still together. Although our daily lives do not intersect, we still regard this unique friendship as a valuable bond. We span three decades in age, and we are in all stages of life – single, married, divorced, empty nesters, children, grandchildren. Over the years, we have really watched the cycle of life unfold before us. And we know we are there for each other.

In the world of elephants, when one elephant is dying, all the other elephants circle around. Our group talks about the elephants circling. When one of us is in need, the others rally around in support. When a 5:00 a.m. call comes, we respond. When my father died, all these women came to his memorial service. Afterward at the reception we all stood in a circle with our arms around each other, and I felt the comfort of connection, I felt their unwavering support and compassion.

My RichLife journey has taught me many lessons. We all learn from different sources – from friends, families, business associates, clients. A great deal of my learning has come through the journeys of my clients. I am not in their lives every day, but I see where they have come from, I see where they are now, and I help them plan for where they want to be in the future.

Being a financial advisor is a great privilege. I work hard to earn my clients' trust as a person who can help them meet their financial goals, and also simply as a person. I treasure the confidence they place in me and my team, and I am humbled by the responsibility that their trust demands of me. It is an honour to work with them, and very satisfying to realize that they, too, are part of my RichLife circle of connection.

Living Well, Living Happy

Living a RichLife, living well, means living happily. It means living with the joy and contentment of having accomplished and experienced as many good things in life as possible.

A motivational speaker once suggested four actions that can help a person find happiness:

- Think about your blessings daily.
- Verbalize your gratitude.
- Shift your focus away from difficulties.
- Lift others in need.

I would add a fifth: act on purpose. Leading a RichLife entails acting intentionally. It means finding your special purpose – call it your vision, your mission, your goal, your dream – and following it with passion.

Chapter 5

GIVING BACK

> *"I really believe it's important to give while you live, so you have the pleasure and satisfaction of knowing where it goes. I don't think of this as a donation, but rather an investment in better health for women in London and southwestern Ontario."*
> - Terrence J. Donnelly, in September 1999, on his gift to establish the Grace Donnelly Women's Health Pavilion in honour of his mother, Grace

Giving back is an important element of the RichLife. Just as there are many ways to live well, there are many ways to give back. And sometimes giving back not only helps others, it also makes us feel good.

Early in 2006, I took my mother to the University Hospital site of the London Health Sciences Centre for a medical appointment. As I entered the building I noticed the above quotation on the wall. I had just been thinking about how wonderful it was to be able to be there with my mother – at another time in my life, I might not have had the time or the opportunity to choose to be with her. Yet here I was.

And here was Terrence Donnelly, another person who obviously honoured his mother, and who had made a contribution that represented more than just money. Oddly enough, his giving back was also a kind of giving ahead, because he made an investment in her future at a time when he could also enjoy the fruits of his contribution.

Sometimes we may not even realize that what we are doing is a way of giving back, and only later do we discover that our actions had a profound effect on another person. One summer I went to a leadership camp called Bark Lake in the Haliburton Highlands in Ontario. It was funded and run by the government, and if the government paid for a camper to attend Bark Lake, the camper had to volunteer at a children's camp for two weeks.

My payback assignment, so to speak, was at Camp Maple Leaf on an island in Pigeon Lake. It was run by a war veterans association for underprivileged children, most of whom came from rough neighbourhoods in Toronto and Hamilton. They were bused to the lake, and then travelled by barge to the camp.

For most of the campers, the brief two-week period they spent there was their first experience in being away from home. And as my first introduction to kids who were from "the other side of the tracks," it was a real eye opener.

At night the campers and I slept in the same cabin. The counsellors had a separate bedroom, but the walls did not go all the way to the ceiling, so I could hear every sound. In my room at night, I would listen to these kids talking about their brothers in jail, about robberies and stabbings. It was unbelievable for me, completely outside my realm of experience.

I realized what a life-changing experience it could be for these kids to be out of a negative environment, to be in a place where nature was just outside the door, where they had three meals a day, and people actually cared about them. They had the opportunity to see things they had never seen and to try activities they had never tried before.

I chose to return to Pigeon Lake the following year and for several summers after that. I could have chosen to work at a private camp, but I chose to go back to Camp Maple Leaf because I believed there was potential to make a difference through this experience. I was a camp counsellor, and I taught swimming.

One summer, I challenged one of the campers to swim to an island in the lake. I agreed to accompany him in a boat as he swam. As he began to tire, he wanted to quit. I knew he was capable of completing the swim, and I told him so. "Float on your back and look up at the sky until you feel rested, then keep swimming. You don't think you can do it, but you can. You'll feel tired at the end. But you'll have the memory of this accomplishment for the rest of your life, long after the tiredness fades away."

I kept in touch with that camper after camp ended and I had gone back to university. His mother had walked out on him and his family, leaving them with their father and no means of support. Essentially he and his siblings were abandoned to fend for themselves. He struck me as being different from the others: he was ambitious and wanted to become a doctor, and he had a good sense of right and wrong.

I used to meet him occasionally for lunch, or at the museum. And I arranged for him to go to Camp Ponacka (the camp takes in one or two children each year on scholarships that are funded by donations). But eventually I lost touch with him.

One day almost twenty years later he was watching a television show about camping in Ontario, and he got in touch with me through a contact number at Camp Ponacka. He said that the time he had spent at the camp completely changed his outlook. He told me that what I had done had stood him in good stead all his life, and that he attributes the transformation of his attitude and his behaviour to my leadership.

I was surprised. I had no idea of the impact our contact had made on him. But he said that when he had returned to the city that summer, he had given up his involvement in petty crime, and he was now proud to be a contributing member of society, with a family he cherished.

He has become a diamond setter and jeweller, and he has made me some beautiful jewellery to show his appreciation. I did not know then the impact I was having, but thankfully, as it turns out, my giving back made a difference.

"I Gave at the Office" Just Doesn't Cut It

When new and prospective clients think about what it would take for them to look back on their lives without regret, many say they want to "make a contribution to society," "do something big," "make the world a better place than it was when I came into it." It may have to do with their stage of life – most of my clients come to me at a time when their basic needs are met, when they are looking to the future, when they are asking themselves what they can do to make a difference – but I am struck by what a recurring theme it is.

In *I'm So Glad You Told Me What I Didn't Want to Hear*, author Barbara Johnson quotes Dr. Karl Menninger, who advised those who felt a nervous breakdown coming on to "lock up your house, go across the railroad tracks, find someone in need and do something to help that person."

There is wisdom in this advice, and it is echoed in the Jewish tradition of *tzedakah*, which reflects a duty to help others in need and to improve the quality of life around us. It is a tradition of charity and social justice that is based on an obligation to give back to those less fortunate than we are. Yes, making a contribution is a consistent theme, but many people have trouble deciding how to make their contribution.

Making a charitable donation for a tax write-off is certainly nobler than trying to hide your money in an LLC in Nevada. But that is not the stuff that giving back is made of. Donations made in the RichLife spirit are donations that are focused on purpose, on what the money can accomplish. Money donated for self-aggrandizement, to garner publicity or fame, or to gain political goodwill certainly serves the recipient. Imagine the feeling of contribution when the donation also serves the passion of the donor!

In fact, recent research shows that doing good deeds can not only make you feel good about yourself, it can actually improve your health and make you happier. According to an article by Erin Anderssen in *The Globe and Mail* (January 15, 2005), several researchers have concluded that people who volunteer their time and energy and who make financial contributions live longer and have improved health when compared with people who do not. So choose how to give back, then dive in and get involved.

Where Do I Contribute?

Pierre Berton was one of the lucky ones who let his passions inform his life as he lived it. Many people never do. And although it may seem dispassionate to use a formal structure to discover or rediscover passion, I like to suggest an organized approach to figure out what people really care about and what their RichLife giveback should look like.

Sue Bochner, a philanthropic advisor who founded the Children's Aid Society Foundation and served as its president for 15 years, has identified eight sections of charitable giving: arts, community/civic, education, environment, health, religion, social service, and sport. She has created a seven-step process to help people discover which of these eight sections they are passionate about. It works like this:

- Develop and make a list of values for your personal charitable program because values help to guide philanthropic choice. What are your core beliefs? What is important to you? Where are you not willing to compromise?

- Choose the sector you are interested in. Charities can be categorized by their activities – the arts, health, sport, to name a few. Which sector seems to grab your attention? Which sector has touched your life in some way? What topical issues do you care about?
- Choose the jurisdiction in which you want to invest your funds. Is it at the local, provincial, national, or international level?
- Determine a cause. Within the geographic area you have chosen and in the sector you have chosen, what is your cause? Is it something long-term, such as medical research or something else in the health sector? Or is it something immediate, such as the emergency relief available at a women's shelter or social service agency?
- Determine a target group. From your list of causes, choose which segment of the population you would like to focus your support on. Do you want to focus on seniors and the need for more and better long-term care facilities, or on physically challenged people and the need to provide them with fuller access to the activities of daily life?
- Choose your charity. Make a list of all the charities that meet your selected criteria; you may need to do research to come up with a comprehensive list.
- Evaluate the charity. Is it worthy of your support? Review the financial statements. Examine the annual reports. Inquire about the organization's expenses-to-revenue ratio (and remember the rule

of thumb that a charity should be spending no more than 20-25% of its total budget on fundraising expenses and administration).

Many people find this decision-tree approach to finding their charitable passion very successful. First they determine what sparks them on a macro level: is it education, health care, arts, environment? Then they decide where they want their contribution to work: is it at the international, national, provincial, or local level? Next they determine how they would like to do the work: through offering their time in hands-on work, wallet work and funding, or best of all, a combination of both. Then they develop a personal matrix of the things they are passionate about, and that objectively helps them decide what their RichLife giveback aspirations are and the unique ways that they want to, and can, make a difference.

You probably have a hot button, too. Do you know what it is? If you already know, that's great. But if you are still trying to figure out what your passion is, then I encourage you to try the seven-step approach. You can learn a lot about what makes a difference to you…and about the kind of difference you want to make.

RichLife Philanthropy: Giving Back with Ongoing Purpose

If charitable giving is about giving back, then philanthropy is about both giving back and leaving a legacy. They are both about passion, certainly. But whereas charitable giving has an impact now and in the relatively short term, philanthropy has a longer-term focus. And philanthropy is about leaving your fingerprints on your contribution.

"You make a living by what you get; you make a life by what you give." This anonymous quotation (often incorrectly attributed to Winston Churchill) could easily be the tag line for the word *philanthropy*. You can make a great living, but unless you're connected to a purpose, your living is really just about your day-to-day existence.

A lot of people do not think seriously about where they would like to give. They contribute to the charities that keep asking for a donation or that offer some sort of quid pro quo. They are "guilted" into saving starving children, or they try to outdo each other with large gifts that invite public acknowledgment. But these types of donations do not express the RichLife spirit of giving.

As I mentioned earlier, I believe that part of my role as a financial advisor is to help people find their passion, and then to help them structure their financial affairs in a way that allows them to pursue that passion in a responsible and intentional way.

Many philanthropists say that they found their passion because of something that touched their lives profoundly. Perhaps they experienced first-hand the tragedy of childhood cancer – either in their own family or in the family of a friend or neighbour – and then became passionate about supporting ongoing research or establishing a fund to send sick kids to camp.

Perhaps they watched as environmental degradation slowly destroyed the lake that had been a family retreat for generations, and then got passionate about environmental issues.

And perhaps the best way to illustrate what I mean by RichLife philanthropy is by telling the stories of people who embody it in the way they give.

Recently, I was fortunate enough to attend a conference called Women Play BIG, presented by the Canadian Women's Foundation and Play BIG. Special guest speakers at this conference on strategic philanthropy included Carol Newell and Doris Buffett.

Carol Newell, an heiress to the Newell Rubbermaid fortune, married a man and moved with him to British Columbia. When Carol arrived there, she fell in love with the mountains, the ocean, the natural beauty of the place. She found her passion in causes related to the local British Columbia environment.

She started a seed capital company to back businesses that are finding ways to stimulate sustainability. She measures return on her investment not by dollars, but more importantly, by the amount of good that is done. She has also created a foundation with the same mission to fund activities and causes that are purely charitable, with no business or profit element to them; her efforts are focused in B.C.

Carol Newell found passion in her local environment. You can approach your giving back in the same way that she did. If you think about how you want to give, if you do it with purpose and intent, if you lay out the parameters of a foundation, citing where donations will be made, and if you stay on track with your goals and guidelines, your giveback will be every bit as organized and influential as hers.

Doris Buffett, sister of Warren Buffett, has created a foundation called The Sunshine Lady Foundation, Inc. A motto of the foundation is, "A Sunshine Lady Foundation grant is a hand-up, not a hand-out." This organization favours giving grants to individuals or small organizations. It prefers to fund specific projects and emergency shortfalls rather than general operating expenses, and issues most grants on a one-time basis.

The Sunshine Lady, Ms. Buffett, is dedicated to breaking cycles of poverty, abuse, and economic dependence through investment in education. Women and children are her first priority; her second is the promotion of philanthropy through education. Her preference is to give matching grants – funding that matches what is raised by the applicant.

The Sunshine Lady Foundation has a group of directors, staff, and volunteers known as Sunbeams who identify opportunities to give that fit with the organization's mandate. The Sunbeams make on-site visits to individuals and small organizations that, because of circumstance, find themselves facing barriers that can be removed by the application of donated funds.

For example, they fund scholarships in specific geographic locations for youth who cannot afford higher education. Ms. Buffett helps them with tuition and expenses, and in return they sign an agreement that they will not drink or do drugs while they are in school.

She sends children to camp and to school. She found a man who had lost his job, and because he could not keep up his car and insurance payments, he could not drive to the job interviews to regain employment. Ms. Buffett helped the man with his car payments so he could attend the interviews. He got a job. She is in the business of enabling people, and she operates on a grassroots, bottom-up basis.

Doris Buffett is very open and clear in her gratitude to her father and her brother for providing the wealth that she uses to accomplish her mission. Doris inherited her wealth, and she uses it as a tool to transform the lives of those with potential and hope for a better future.

No story that is written in Canada about giving back would be complete without mention of Kenneth Thomson, Canada's wealthiest man until his death in June 2006. For much of his life he was not noted as a public benefactor, although he did donate $4.5 million in 1982 to the construction of the famous Toronto concert hall that he then named after his father, Roy Thomson, and another $5 million in 2000 for renovation of the venue. But it is reported that he liked to give money without fanfare in "droplets of $100,000 here and there" to organizations whose work he supported.

But it was in 2002 that he made history with the bequest of most of his art collection to the Art Gallery of Ontario. Mr. Thomson was an art lover throughout his life, and he had put together a collection that rivals the best in the world. It was valued at $300 million at the time of the bequest. He gave an additional $70 million to the AGO, $50 million to be used toward the expansion and renovation of the gallery and $20 million for operations.

This was truly giving back in a big way, and his giveback has now become a part of his legacy – an ongoing legacy to the many people whose lives will be enriched by these wonderful works of art, and a legacy that confirms Toronto's place as a leading centre for the arts.

Kenneth Thomson was able to make such generous contributions because of his enormous wealth. And many hundreds of thousands of people will benefit from his generosity over the years. But perhaps the most eloquent expression of what he gave back while he was alive is this passage from an article that appeared the day after he died:

> Among many legacies he left yesterday after his unexpected death at the age of 82 – controlling shareholder of The Globe and Mail, a vast empire of electronic media businesses, oil and gas assets in the North Sea, the largest fortune in Canada and the ninth largest in the world – is the human example he set.
>
> He was hard evidence that an enlightened billionaire can exist. His fate was to be an uncommonly wealthy man, and an almost accidental tycoon. But his deepest interest

lay in reminding himself and others what it is to be human, and what we have in common.
(Ian Brown and Sandra Martin, *The Globe and Mail*, June 13, 2006)

Making significant gifts is part of the currency of social capital. And the right person making the right contribution at the right time with the right approach and the right purpose can change the world. Even if it is only a little at a time. Sonja Cohen's story is a perfect example of this.

Giving Back with More than Money

Sonja and Karl Cohen (not their real names) stayed actively engaged with the world and with each other throughout their entire life. Up until Sonja's death, they were almost inseparable. They shared so many experiences and so many challenges that they were almost closer than you could imagine two people to be. They each brought different kinds of support to their relationship. Karl cared for Sonja through her bouts of depression, and as they aged, Sonja was the one who remained more mobile and able to look after day-to-day tasks.

Let me tell you a story that exemplifies Sonja's generosity and her commitment to life. She and Karl were survivors of the Holocaust. They brought little with them when they fled from Europe, but Sonja had managed to hold onto some old-fashioned patterns for knit dolls. Sonja used to knit beautiful dolls from these patterns, and when she sold a doll, she donated the money to one of her favourite charities.

I purchased some dolls from her, and rather than take the money she asked me to write a cheque for what I thought they were worth and send it to the Alzheimer's Society. The people who received Sonja's dolls as gifts found them especially meaningful.

The dolls became Sonja's way of giving back and they became her legacy. She combined her time, her skill of knitting, and her love of people into a RichLife contribution that she was able to continue to the end of her life, even from her chair in the nursing home where she lived her final days.

Sonja's giveback was her talent to create beautiful dolls and her encouragement to those who loved them to donate to a charitable cause. The dolls themselves are a giveback because they will continue to give pleasure to those who are lucky enough to have one, and the donations are another giveback. But giving back really does not have to be about money at all. It can simply be giving your time, your support, or your service in a quiet way.

Susan is a good friend and also a member of Women in the Wilderness. She has always given of herself whenever the opportunity arose. Susan's niece developed cancer several years ago, and Susan spent a lot of her time guiding her niece through this experience, taking her to the doctor, going for tests, offering any kind of support that her niece needed. The cancer recurred twice, requiring two separate stem cell transplants, and each time Susan was able to drop what she was doing to help out. Currently, the cancer is in remission, and her niece is able to live a more independent life.

And then a short time ago, Susan got a call from a friend in the Bahamas. The friend's husband was terminally ill. Susan packed up her things and went down to support her friend through this difficult time.

Susan is fortunate enough to have the financial resources that allow her to put her own life "on hold" while she serves her friends and family. But she also finds time for other things that are important to her. A few years ago Susan took up art: she is painting, participating in art shows, and selling her paintings. She is following her passion. She is financially able to turn her life to what she likes and wants to do. Susan has a RichLife.

Some people may be able to give back in ways that affect thousands of people, and others may be able to give back in ways that affect only their immediate family. But no person's life is better than another's based solely on the financial value of what they are able to give. We try to live our lives in the best way we can. And I believe we have an obligation to look for ways to be good stewards in this life – to leave this world a better, richer place than it was when we entered.

Chapter 6

LEAVING A LEGACY

We all leave some kind of legacy behind. We leave it in the hearts and minds and memories of our children and grandchildren and of all the people whose lives we have touched. We leave our mark in every home we have built, in every community we have lived, in everything we have accomplished.

How will you be remembered? Your legacy represents your whole life; it is more than the physical property and financial assets you have amassed during your lifetime. Your legacy is your character, your successes, your relationships. Your legacy can be your work, as it was for Marie Curie, Louis Pasteur, Pierre Trudeau, Pierre Berton. It can be a monument, a rose window in a church, a hospital room, a park, a planted tree. Your legacy can be a fellowship, an endowment, a new library or a new library book.

I have seen people leave legacies rich with meaning and impact. I have seen others leave legacies of pain and strife. The biggest lesson I have learned is that those who leave the most valuable legacies are the ones who have paid attention to their passion and who have been consistently intentional in how they want to be remembered. And I have also learned that each of us has the opportunity to choose our way.

Your Legacy: Passive or Planned?

Many people leave legacies they are not even aware of – witness the many artists who were penniless when they died, yet whose works command millions of dollars at auctions today. Did Michelangelo know as he painted it that the work he produced on the ceiling of the Sistine Chapel would have such lasting significance?

Some leave an accidental legacy. Take, for example, Sir Arthur Conan Doyle, the author of the heralded Sherlock Holmes mysteries. That is certainly how I remember him, don't you? Conan Doyle dreamed of becoming a successful author, and his dream came true, though certainly not in the way that he had envisioned: he wanted to be recognized as the author of serious, meaningful works. But at the age of 28, he introduced his now famous detective to the world in his first mystery book, *A Study in Scarlet*.

Despite his best intentions, Conan Doyle became so well known for Sherlock Holmes that few people paid attention to his other writings. He never considered his Holmes stories to be significant, yet with them he achieved success as the writer of the most popular detective fiction of his day. And he left the world an "accidental" legacy of Sherlock Holmes mysteries.

Some people, unfortunately, leave an unintentional legacy of strife and discord. Here is a case in point. I have two clients who own an interior design business. The lot that the bricks and mortar store sits on is an extremely valuable piece of real estate. These two people are inextricably linked as owners of the property, and there are three others who also have an interest in it. When I talk to them, they say their families are their most important consideration. They love their children and their grandchildren; they want to take care of their families. But the children are not interested in the store or the business, and their only interest in the property is in the value it will bring when it is finally sold.

The biggest gift these clients could give would be to liquidate the property and make comprehensive estate plans so the children do not get embroiled in a messy dispute over distribution of assets. The clients think that leaving the property to the children will hold them together, but speaking from the perspective of years of experience, I think this unintentional legacy will have the opposite effect. It is a time bomb ticking quietly until the clients' deaths will cause it to explode.

But it can be done differently. Some people plan carefully to leave a RichLife legacy. My own mother is an example of such a person. She wanted to be sure that the harmony among her children would not be disturbed by her death and the subsequent division of assets. So my mother called the four children together. She told us that her biggest goal was for everyone to continue to get along after she was gone. She said, "I will do everything I can, make as many decisions now as I can, to ensure that that happens."

She told us how she would like to live out her life, how she would like her funeral to be conducted, and how she would make decisions about who gets what now. Part of the meeting was very practical: the job of allocating assets is much easier if it is planned. And my mother wanted to be sure that each of us received the things that had particular meaning for us. She wanted us to remain bonded together in celebration of her life, not to be divided by discord at her death. I wish more people had the foresight to do things the way she did.

Let me share with you also the story of clients of mine who exemplify the three elements of the RichLife. Wilma and Jim Spence are now in their seventies. I have watched them over the years as they have worked together to lead a RichLife. And they have done it right.

They live well. They have built a strong relationship. They are close to each other as spouses, partners, and friends. Together they attend the theatre and the symphony. They travel together. They take university courses together. And they each pursue their own separate interests as well. They maintain their individuality, and they complement one another well.

Wilma and Jim have helped their children and grandchildren with their educations. They have a cottage where all three generations of their family often congregate. And they often have more formal family reunions that may see them travelling together as one big extended family to more distant places such as Alaska and South Africa.

They have contributed to their community through their work in both the corporate world and the social service sector. They volunteer. They serve on boards.

The Spences live well. They give back. And they will leave a legacy. They will leave an intangible legacy of leadership and of character. And they will leave a tangible legacy through their estate plan. Wilma and Jim have not amassed a huge fortune, but they have used their resources wisely, and they have created a true RichLife legacy.

The Richardson Family: Living Their Legacy

Let me start this section with a caveat: I work for one of the Richardson family businesses, Richardson Partners Financial Limited, and I am a member of the board of directors. But I include the story of the Richardson family here because I really cannot think of a better example of careful planning to ensure an ongoing legacy. Their planning for the future encompasses both succession planning for the successful stewardship of their business interests and philanthropic planning to support a variety of causes they have identified as priorities.

In 2007, James Richardson & Sons Limited of Winnipeg will celebrate its 150th year as a business owned and operated by the Richardson family. Its operations encompass agriculture, financial services, oil and gas exploration, and property management. Apart from running their businesses successfully, the Richardsons also developed comprehensive wealth planning and management services – including tax plans, estate plans, succession plans, family trusts, and philanthropic foundations – to meet their family's needs and circumstances.

In 2003, they took this to the next level and founded a firm dedicated to serving the particular needs of very wealthy families. They knew what kind of financial management they wanted for themselves, and they created this business as a vehicle to ensure that not only they, but also others in similar circumstances, could access the specialized products, services, and expertise they need.

Many family fortunes are made and lost in three generations. But the Richardsons have avoided that unfortunate fate: their family business now spans six generations. And they have created a model that could be applied to any family business to ensure that it does not fall victim to second- or third-generation failure. This model itself is a part of their legacy to others because through Richardson Partners Financial Limited they are willing to share the secrets of their success so that other families in business may also continue to thrive.

One element of this model is that any Richardson family members who want to join the firm have to complete their education and prove themselves in another arena first; they have to apply for employment just as other people do; and they have to roll up their sleeves and work with dedication, just like anyone else who wants to get ahead.

One of the Richardsons remembers shovelling grain and cleaning out silos in a grain elevator on the Prairies. He says it was the best way to learn what an honest, hard day's work means – and it was great preparation for working in the family business.

Yes, the Richardsons have been extremely successful at business and at maintaining and growing their business interests over many generations. But their success has not created in them a sense of entitlement. Rather, they live with a sense of the responsibility that their wealth entails.

The family members often quote their grandmother, who used to like to remind them of the familiar adage, "To whomsoever much is given, much is is also required." She meant it. The family allocates a certain percentage of corporate profits for charitable giving through the Richardson Foundation, the engine of their philanthropic legacy. They have identified the areas of charitable giving that they are passionate about, and have streamlined the decision-making process by clearly setting forth the criteria that a charity must meet to qualify for a donation.

The Richardson family story is truly a RichLife story – one of creating, preserving, growing, and transferring their wealth from generation to generation, and of doing good things with it all along the way.

What Will Your Legacy Be About?

> *"For most of us, we will be remembered far more briefly. In the end, as we reflect on the meaning of our lives and our legacy to the future, what more could we ask for than to be remembered with affection and respect by a few people who will survive a decade or two further, by our children and grandchildren?"* David Suzuki. *David Suzuki: The Autobiography*

People choose how they would like to leave their legacy in the same way they choose how they want to give back. Most start with their families, with their children and grandchildren. When they have provided for both the present and future needs of their families, they look at how they can contribute to other people in their lives and in their communities. They may contribute to education, to health care, to the environment, to cultural agencies. Then they may look to larger communities, to their town or city, to their province, to the nation, and finally to the international community.

They leave formal legacies through wills and philanthropic giving, and they leave informal legacies through the way they lived their lives. People want to make a difference in whatever way they can. Witness the legacy that Terry Fox left when he ran his gruelling course across the country to raise money for cancer research, the tenacity of those who fought to preserve the Rouge River watershed from encroaching development, and the Amber Alert that mobilizes an entire nation to be on the watch for a child who has been abducted.

It has been said that one of the greatest gifts a person can give is to plant trees under which he or she will never enjoy the shade, and some people do. People leave legacies that affect the environment, some through hands-on work, some through donations. They are forward-looking, trying to preserve the natural environment for the generations that will follow.

People leave legacies that preserve culture and support cultural achievement. For instance, Michael Lee-Chin contributed generously to support the major renovation of and addition to the Royal Ontario Museum, and upon its completion the dramatic Michael Lee-Chin Crystal (scheduled to open in May 2007) will be an architectural icon of

Toronto. And let us not forget the contributions of those whose money built places such as Massey Hall in Toronto and the Ivor Wynn stadium in Hamilton, venues that have already been enjoyed by thousands of people over many decades.

People leave huge legacies in the field of health and wellness. Spurred by a personal medical tragedy or by seeming miracles, some people have a strong desire to make a difference for others. So they contribute entire hospital wings, or research centres, or MRI machines. Or perhaps they have been touched by poverty and hunger, and they help establish and operate food banks so that others might have a chance to receive better nutrition.

People leave legacies in the field of education: university endowments or establishment of research chairs, memorial scholarships or educational grants that help someone receive an education they would not otherwise be able to afford.

Another Camp Ponacka story. My father remembered that in times of war people would help each other without asking questions, often without even knowing each other's names. So he started a tradition at camp that created an ongoing memorial. He painted the words "The Unknown Gentleman" on a huge rock in a clearing in the woods. To this day, every group of campers is required to gather at this rock once during their stay at the camp. The campers walk through the woods to the rock, each carrying a smaller rock. One by one the campers come up and tell a real story about either being an unknown gentleman or being the recipient of a random act of kindness from an unknown gentleman – or gentlewoman. The camper leaves the rock in a pile that has formed around the monster boulder.

There are more than fifty years worth of rocks piled around that Unknown Gentleman, all evidence of legacies left. Reminders of simple legacies that meant something special to one individual.

And my father left another, more personal legacy. Before he died, he created a time capsule, and my mother, my son, and I went with him to bury it at the rock of the Unknown Gentleman. When my son turns 70, he is to return to the camp and recover that time capsule. In it he will discover a newspaper, notes, coins, and letters, all designed to mark the passage of time, to remind of past history, to rekindle memories.

Tell Your Story Well

There is a company called StoryBook Films in Toronto that produces personal history documentaries. Their tag line is "Every Life Makes a Compelling Story." Their service is their business: documenting the life of an individual or of a family.

They capture on film interviews with the client and their family and friends. Then they edit the film, and they add both narration and music to produce a professional biography. They capture the client's story for future generations. And they do it because they believe that the stories told by mom and dad, grandma and grandpa, give us context for where we have come from and for who we are. They want to preserve those stories, and the success of their venture depends upon people wanting to preserve their stories, too. I think they're onto something.

Before the days of print and electronic media, people preserved their history by telling stories. They gathered together and reminisced about the good times, told yarns to make people laugh, and told stories to warn the younger folk of dangers and alert them to opportunities. Even today, families are brought together as soon as someone says, "Remember the time…?" Your story is your life. Your life is your legacy. No matter what you plan or intend or forecast or dream, what actually happens is what will be written in the minds and hearts of the people left behind.

We all leave a legacy. What kind of legacy do you want to leave? What will people say when they remember you?

Chapter 7

THE RICHLIFE ADVISOR: PRACTICAL PLANNING, INTIMATE COUNSEL

It was not too long ago that to be a financial advisor to individual clients meant being a stockbroker, and stockbrokers were basically salespeople who earned their living through the commissions they could generate selling stocks and bonds to their clients, many of whom did not really understand what they were buying.

One of the benefits of this electronic age is that it has brought with it not only a virtual explosion of information but also easy access to that information. As a result, many investors have become more knowledgeable about their finances.

At the same time, the educational and professional development standards in the investment industry have become more stringent, and advisors now have ample opportunity and a duty to develop a sophisticated understanding of financial markets, investment strategies, and the wide array of available financial products. The ones who take advantage of this opportunity are as different from the old stockbroker as a Ph.D. is from a Grade 6 graduation certificate.

I consider it a privilege to be a financial advisor. It is a position of intimate counsel, and it brings with it the responsibility of talking with my clients about the things that are most important to them.

Asking my clients about their finances is a given. But in order for the financial information to make sense, I need to understand the context of their lives. I talk to my clients about their health, about their family relationships, business issues, personal issues.

I need to understand where they have come from and their vision of where they want to go. Most clients do not consider these questions nosy or taboo; they understand that their investments should be structured in a way that reflects both their financial and their non-financial priorities.

I understand that being a financial advisor puts me in a unique position. It is a position that I appreciate and value and treat with the respect it deserves. As an advisor, I have the responsibility of understanding my clients' motivations and priorities, and when clients are not quite certain about these, I have the opportunity of helping them clarify what their motivations and priorities are.

Everyone has a vision, a dream of what they want their lives to be. In the process of helping my clients achieve their financial goals, I know I also help them realize their dreams. And in doing this, I am also reaching mine.

The Three Ts of Do-It-Yourself Investing: Time, Temperament, and Talent

Some people manage their own investments. Some do it with great success, some do it adequately, and others struggle all along the way. Investment "do-it-yourselfers" often fall into what I call "the amateur golfer syndrome." You have probably known golfers who spend hours at the driving range, practising drives off the tee. They seem to forget that golf is a whole game – sure, it starts with the tee-off, but after that successful play depends on good strategy and execution of the long drives and the short game of chips and putts.

Investors can fall into a similar trap. They can become focused, for instance, on the challenge and excitement of picking stocks and then lose sight of how their stock purchases are affecting the balance of their portfolio as a whole. They seem to forget about the strategy that should be guiding all their investment decisions.

If people are not successful at handling their own investments, I do not think it is necessarily their fault. To manage money well, you need what I refer to as the "Three Ts" – time, temperament, and talent. The time to devote to the activity of financial management. The temperament to walk the tightrope between greed and fear. The talent to pursue knowledge and understanding of investment management.

Sound financial management requires a great deal of focused and dedicated time. Time to learn about investment markets and investment products. Time to understand the many different investment strategies that are available today – and when to use them. Time to form relationships with people who can mentor you, and time to figure out who can offer the soundest advice and support. You need time to make mistakes and learn from them. And when you have invested all this time, you need the time to structure your investments properly and to monitor them regularly.

People who manage their own finances need the kind of temperament that allows them to establish carefully-thought-out investment priorities. They need to be dispassionate about their investments. They need the kind of temperament that allows them consistently to make objective investment decisions based on the priorities they have established. They need to be clear about both their short-term and their long-term investment objectives, and comfortable with the balance of risk and reward that will help them meet those objectives.

They cannot fall in love with the hopes and dreams that the "stories" of their stock picks inevitably contain. They need the fortitude to stick to their plan and not get caught up in the tumult of fear and greed that causes so many people to switch back and forth between investments that are too risky and investments that are too conservative.

And what about talent? When we see professional athletes or entertainers performing well, we often remark that they seem to make what they are doing seem effortless. We know that their performance looks easy only because they have worked so hard to master their craft. And we also recognize that even all their hard work could never produce such a performance if they did not have an inherent talent to begin with.

Some people have a talent for investment management, others do not. It is a combination of knowledge and ability – a knack for reading situations and events in a certain way. And it needs to be nurtured through hard work, through acquiring specific knowledge about economics and market dynamics, and through experience.

...and Two People Who Chose Not To Go It Alone

Let me tell you a couple of client stories to illustrate the point that if you are missing even one of the Three Ts, you would do well to consider how a financial professional might give you more peace of mind about your affairs.

Charlotte is a great example of someone who did not have all of the Three Ts. She had plenty of time to invest in her finances, but she was overwhelmed by the constant flow of paperwork – trade confirmations, investment account statements, bank statements, quarterly and annual reports from companies whose securities she held. Her solution was simply to ignore the paper.

In fact, when she came to see me she had three years worth of unopened envelopes in a box. Charlotte was relieved when I told her that I could help her sort out her affairs, and we soon got her on the right track. She had the time, and she may have had the talent, but she definitely did not have the temperament to tackle the job.

Some time later Charlotte told me that her ex-husband was planning to sell his company. She was worried because she did not understand how the impending sale might affect her financial situation. She confided in me about the financial terms of her divorce, and I was able to show her exactly what the sale would mean.

Again, she was relieved. I am not a lawyer, a counsellor, or a therapist, but I was able to bring perspective to her situation through a financial analysis that she simply did not have the knowledge to perform.

If Charlotte lacked the temperament to handle her own money, John lacked the time. John was a financial professional who managed hundreds of millions of dollars for large institutional investors such a pension funds. I first met him when I was on the institutional side of the business, and I had always admired him. He was extremely capable – a financial wizard, really.

I ran into him shortly after I moved to the private client side of the investment world, and I told him what I was up to. John was thrilled. He told me he really needed someone to help with his own investments because he worked so hard for his clients that he did not have enough time to handle his personal investments properly. He managed large organizational investments expertly, but he was so focused on his clients' portfolios that he found it difficult to focus on his own needs.

It was a classic example of the shoemaker's children not having shoes – a not uncommon phenomenon in the world of finance. John asked me to help him, so I began to manage his personal investments, and when he was planning to retire, I helped him make decisions about restructuring his investments for this new phase of his life. John is retired now, and I am happy to say that he continues to rely on my financial management and advice even though he could look after his own affairs if he wanted to.

Relationship and RichLife Advice

Financial management is a combination of skill and art. I recently saw an advertisement for the Investment Management Consultants Association telling us that "to expertly advise the very wealthy, you need a split personality. Part tax advisor, part estate planner, part financial genius and part shrink." Then it goes on to address the life cycle of wealth – accumulation, preservation/protection, and distribution.

Do you notice what is missing? That's right, the "shrink" connection. I do not claim to be a "shrink," I do not want to be one, and I certainly do not think that my clients' wealth means they need one. But I do believe very strongly that when my clients invite me to do so, I have a responsibility as their financial advisor, as someone who knows their dreams and goals, to provide counsel about both the financial and non-financial issues that are important in their lives.

Dan Sullivan of The Strategic Coach® has outlined a brief history of financial advice. In 1885, financial advice consisted of determining which commodities to buy and sell to make a profit. By 1974, financial advisors were focusing on which products were best suited to their clients' needs.

Less than a decade later, financial planning emerged as advisors began to help their clients develop explicit short-term and long-term goals, and strategies to take advantage of unprecedented deregulation and high interest rates. In 1999, with ethical scandals rocking the financial world, client focus shifted once again.

People began to see that their financial plans and their life plans should be aligned. And financial advisors began taking on the role of helping their clients with life planning – helping them to define what is important to them, understanding their values, their goals and dreams, and then structuring their financial affairs with these in mind. That is the type of advisor-client relationship that is the foundation of my practice, the foundation of this book, and the foundation of the RichLife.

Here is an example of how I use relationship to help my clients find their RichLife. One focus of my practice is helping people cope with the unfamiliar demands of what I call "sudden wealth." Examples of sudden wealth include people who have worked hard to build a business from the ground up and then sell that business. They find themselves with huge financial assets and with no clue as to how to handle this suddenly acquired wealth. They are often feeling a bit disoriented, too, because they no longer have work to do and they miss the sense of identity that work provides.

These people are in need of advice they can trust, advice that comes from someone who has a genuine interest in them as individuals. I think these people deserve to enjoy the fruits of their labour. But many of them have had to watch their finances closely all their lives, and they find it difficult to comprehend the many choices their new-found wealth offers them. I love introducing the concept of the RichLife to these clients. It often opens up a whole new world for them.

Regardless of where their money comes from, my clients all share a common characteristic when they come to me for advice. All of them have enough money to live comfortably and to leave their families financially secure.

Unfortunately, the similarities end there. I say "unfortunately" because many of my clients, even in middle and late adulthood, have never quite figured out what they want their money to do for them. Some still live as though their financial resources were limited. Some still focus all their energy on acquiring more wealth.

They represent a happy challenge for me because as their financial advisor, I know I want to take them from The R-Factor Questions to the RichLife. And I trust that our developing relationship – and their developing trust – will allow me to do that. And I have every confidence that their lives will be fuller and happier when they decide they want to Live Well, Give Back, and Leave a Legacy.

THE LAST WORD

You must be the change you want to see in the world.
- Mahatma Gandhi

On our gravestones, two dates will be marked: the day we are born and the day we die. Our lives take place in the small dash that separates those dates. We are all somewhere in our dash…and I hope this book will contribute to your RichLife journey as you travel between these two significant dates.

We each define our own success. We can evaluate our priorities. We can write our own obituaries, and then live up to them. We can imagine how our grandchildren will talk about us, and then we can change if we want them to say something different. Just like Ebenezer Scrooge in Charles Dickens' *A Christmas Carol*, we have the opportunity to see into the future, envision what we want it to be, and then to plan for it, and make our dream a reality.

I have learned so much in my years as a financial professional, and as I have planned and created these pages I have had the opportunity to review many important lessons.

I have learned that the RichLife is not just about money, but that money can be an invaluable enabler of the RichLife.

I have realized that making, keeping, and growing wealth can be an honourable objective, especially when it is done with the thought of how that wealth can be used to create a better experience of life for ourselves and for others.

I have realized anew that my goal as a financial advisor is not only to maximize my clients' wealth, but to help them determine how that wealth will shape their lives.

I have learned that it is important for people to enjoy the rewards of their hard work, to have the kind of life that serves both their needs and their passions. For some, living well means having enough money to give some of it away, to travel, to have more than one pair of eyeglasses. For others it means being healthy, enjoying work instead of dreading it, having satisfying relationships with family and friends. It means finally banishing the worry that kept them on edge and sometimes left them sleepless. Living well is physical, mental, emotional, spiritual, and financial comfort.

I have learned that it is important to give back, and that giving back feels good. You can give back to your family, to your community, to your city or to your country, or to people whose lives may have been touched by something that touched yours – illness, accident, tragedy, or love.

I have learned that no matter what people do, they leave a legacy. It may be a legacy they intended to leave, or it may be an unintended legacy. Their legacy may be as lasting as an opera house or museum wing, or it may be as ephemeral as how they are remembered by their family and their friends. And I have learned that it is almost always better to be intentional about what you want your legacy to be.

I have learned that money is important, but that we need to make sure it is worth more than the paper on which it is printed.

In closing, I would like to leave you with three wishes. You can probably guess what they are -

Live Well - work hard, enjoy a good lifestyle and a good life.

Give Back - work smart, and use your wealth to make the world a better place.

Leave a Legacy - build something that you can be proud of and that your family and friends will be proud of after you are gone.

Let us all strive to live the RichLife.

ACKNOWLEDGEMENTS

There are so many people who have inspired me over the years with the ideas that underpin my RichLife philosophy. My heartfelt thanks go out to the following for the help they have given me, knowingly or unknowingly, in writing this book.

To my clients in my wealth management practice, who have challenged me to provide sound financial advice and allowed me to help them connect their financial resources with their life purpose. Thank you for selecting The Latremoille Group when you have many other choices.

To my professional team members who make up The Latremoille Group – Anne O'Farrell, Jody Bent, Tracy Gascoine and Penny McClure – thank you for your partnership on a daily basis in serving the diverse and individual needs of our loyal clients, and in helping us grow to be one of the leading financial advisory teams in Canada.

To The Richardson Family for their vision in creating Richardson Partners Financial Ltd. – Canada's first independent firm to dedicate itself to Family Wealth Management in its most holistic form. And to Sandy Riley, Sue Dabarno, my fellow board members, and the whole team at RPFL for their ongoing support.

To my collaborators in The Sudden Wealth Solution – Peter Creaghan, Steve Landau, and Pearl Schusheim – for helping to build resources for people facing huge change in their professional, financial, and personal lives.

To Dan Sullivan and Babs Smith of The Strategic Coach, who constantly kindle my entrepreneurial fires and encourage me as a financial advisor to do my part to transform our industry.

To the members of my Goal Cultivator Community who helped me to change my doubts about the project into the courage to speak by getting me to ask myself, "If not me and now, then who and when?"

To all the teachers, Wendy, Bernie, Elissa, and Xenia, and to the Kripalu Yoga Centre, for helping me study and practice yoga for many years. Many of the spiritual elements in my book stem from this discipline.

To Sue Bochner who helped start me on my journey in philanthropy at the Children's Aid Society Foundation, and who continues to be a Leave-a-Legacy champion.

To my friends Pam and Gillian, and to The Women in the Wilderness – Tina, Linda, Carole, Susan, and Nadine – who have given me reason over the past 23 years to step back from my daily routine simply to connect in friendship.

To my personal-life team members who make it possible for me to manage the sometimes competing demands of being a mother, wife, friend, professional, leader, and healthy woman – Tanya, Kati, Victor, Gig, Sarah C., Kim, Suzanne, and Bari.

To Elsa Franklin, a long-time client and publicist, who encouraged me to put my thoughts and ideas into book form, and who got the project going. To Bruce MacDougall, who penned my initial thoughts. To the visionary leadership of the Metris Group team, under which the project took shape: Ross Slater supported my vision; Catherine Nanton and Tom Churchill spent countless hours refining my ideas and stories; Suzanne Noga created the cover illustration; Olena Sullivan designed the book; Jennifer Tribe managed the entire project; and many others too numerous to name helped make this happen.

Finally, to my family, especially to my parents Gwen and Bruno Morawetz, to my aunt Margit Meissner, and to my siblings Anne, Tom, and Tim. To my husband Greg Latremoille who supports and tolerates my hive of never-ending activity. To my stepchildren Maxine and Jason who have taught me that a blended family is a real family. And last but not least, to my children Nicholas and Sarah who are such an important part of my RichLife and my legacy.

ABOUT THE AUTHOR

Susan Latremoille is an investment professional with more than 20 years of experience in the industry. She worked on the institutional side of the business as a vice president at Merrill Lynch Canada. In the late 1980s, she moved to the private client side of the business at RBC Dominion Securities, where she served on and chaired the firm's Private Client Advisory Board (1997 to 1999) and was a member of the firm's prestigious Chairman's Council for 10 years.

The Latremoille Group was founded in 1990 to provide an unprecedented level of financial management, investment advice, and personalized service to her clients. Since 2004 she has been a Wealth Advisor at Richardson Partners Financial Limited, where she is a First Vice President and a member of the Richardson Financial Group Limited Board of Directors.

Susan believes her role as a financial advisor is to help her clients find the perfect equilibrium between fear and greed, risk and return, growth and income, worry and confidence. She knows that this balance is different for each individual, and that is why candid relationships form the basis of her practice. Retirement planning, estate planning, insurance planning, tax planning, and establishment of appropriate corporate structures are among the services that allow Susan to adopt a comprehensive approach to the management of her clients' financial assets. Nothing gives her greater pleasure than helping her clients use their wealth to create full and fulfilling lives.

She was recognized for excellence among Investment Advisors in 1999 when she received the Investment Dealers Association of Canada's *Award of Distinction* for Ontario. She is a fellow of the Canadian Securities Institute; she achieved the Portfolio Manager designation in 2001; and she holds a Level II Insurance licence. Susan earned her MBA from the Canadian School of Management and her BA from the University of Toronto.

Susan is active in the industry as a member of Women in Capital Markets and the Investment Managers Consultants Association. She is also a former member of the Women's Presidents' Organization, a forum for highly successful Canadian businesswomen.

As a philanthropist, Susan is A Leading Woman with the United Way and a member of the Canadian Women's Foundation 100. She is a past board member of the Children's Aid Society Foundation of Metropolitan Toronto. She contributes to the community through her volunteer and financial support of various charitable organizations.

Susan lives in Toronto with her husband Greg Latremoille and their two children Nicholas and Sarah.

You may order copies of The RichLife

directly from our website at

www.TheLatremoilleGroup.com